Hello Reader!
Picture
Dictionary

Hello Reader!

Picture Dictionary ®

Compiled by Gina Shaw and Kimberly Weinberger
Advisor: Peggy Intrator

Illustrators:
Ron Fritz, Patti Goodnow,
Cristina Ong, Marcy Dunn Ramsey

Cartwheel
·B·O·O·K·S· ®

SCHOLASTIC INC.

New York   Toronto   London   Auckland   Sydney   Mexico City   New Delhi   Hong Kong

ISBN 0-590-03547-9

Ron Fritz—pp. 22-23, 26-27, 34-35, 36-37, 38-39, 46-47, 54-55, 68-69, 76-77.
Patti Goodnow—pp. 8-9, 10-11, 12-13, 42-43, 48-49, 50-51, 72-73, 82-83, 84-85.
Cristina Ong—pp. 14-15, 24-25, 28-29, 30-31, 32-33, 40-41, 44-45, 64-65, 70-71, 78-79, 80-81.
Marcy Dunn Ramsey—pp. 16-17, 18-19, 20-21, 52-53, 56-57, 58-59, 60-61, 62-63, 66-67, 74-75.

10 9 8 7 6 5 4 3 2 1   9/9   00 01 02 03 04

Printed in the U.S.A.   24
First printing, September 1999

The *Hello Reader! Picture Dictionary* has been designed to help build children's vocabulary by introducing them to over 650 descriptive words. Based on words in the **Hello Reader!** easy-to-read series of books, this dictionary is sure to help children improve their language skills as they identify familiar pictures in the book.

The words have been organized into 39 themes. Each theme has its own two-page spread. The spread includes a full-color illustration with numbered objects. In the border surrounding each illustration, pictures of the numbered objects are shown in isolation right next to the correct vocabulary word. Children can name the objects they know in the big picture and then check their answers in the border. There is a complete index of all the words at the back of the book.

This book should be especially helpful to those children who are just learning English as well as those children who are just learning to read.

Table of Contents

Letters of the Alphabet

Aa Bb C
Ff Gg Hh
Li Mm N
Qq Rr S
Vv Ww X

c Dd Ee

Ii Jj Kk

n Oo Pp

s Tt Uu

x Yy Zz

Numbers 1-10

1 sun

2 bikes

3 dogs

4 balls

5 birds

6 kites

7 clouds

8 umbrellas

9 ducks

10 turtles

(1) one

(2) two

(3) three

(4) four

(5) five

(6) six

(7) seven

(8) eight

(9) nine

(10) ten

Numbers 11-20

11
sailboats

12
clocks

13
ice cream cones

14
strawberries

15
fish

16 bees

17 flowers

18 ladybugs

19 snails

20 stars

(11) eleven

(12) twelve

(13) thirteen

(14) fourteen

(15) fifteen

(16) sixteen

(17) seventeen

(18) eighteen

(19) nineteen

(20) twenty

Colors

1. blue
2. brown
3. red
4. yellow
5. pink
6. purple
7. black
8. white
9. green
10. orange

15

Family

 ①  me

 ②  sister

 ③  mommy

(4) baby brother  (5) daddy (6) brother

(7) grandma

(8) grandpa

(9) uncle

(10) aunt

(11) great-aunt

(12) cousin

Feelings

 1 happy

 2 sad

 3 angry

 4 scared

 5 calm

 6 shy

 7 brave

 8 excited

 9 proud

10 sorry

19

Parts of the Body

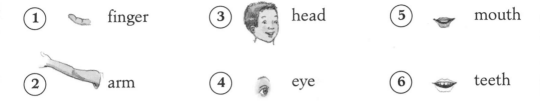

1. finger
2. arm
3. head
4. eye
5. mouth
6. teeth

(7) back

(9) nose

(11) ankle

(8) stomach

(10) hand

(12) shoulder

(13) ear

(14) neck

(15) knee

(16) hair

(17) leg

(18) nail

(19) foot

(20) toe

Clothes

1 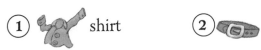 shirt   2 belt   3 jeans

(4) cap   (5) button   (6) pants

(7) socks

(8) dress

(9) shoes

(10) blouse

(11) skirt

(12) t-shirt

(13) leggings

(14) vest

(15) sneakers

23

Bedroom

(1) door

(3) hanger

(5) shade

(2) bathrobe

(4) mirror

(6) window

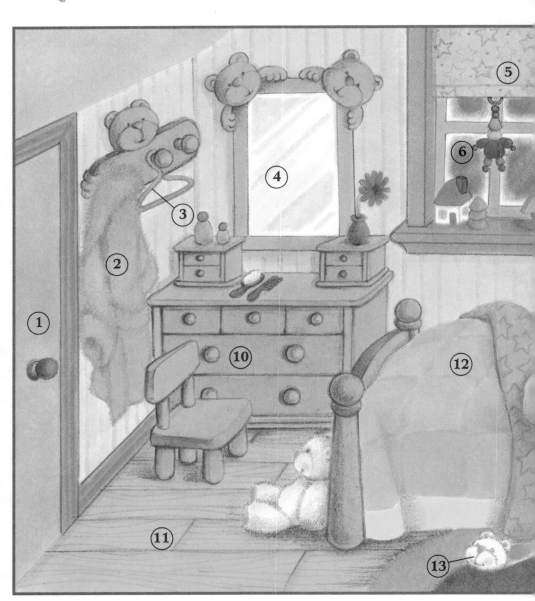

(7) lamp

(9) ceiling

(11) floor

(8) wall

(10) dresser

(12) blanket

(13) slipper

(14) pajamas

(15) sheet

(16) pillow

(17) bed

(18) rug

(19) drawer

(20) clock

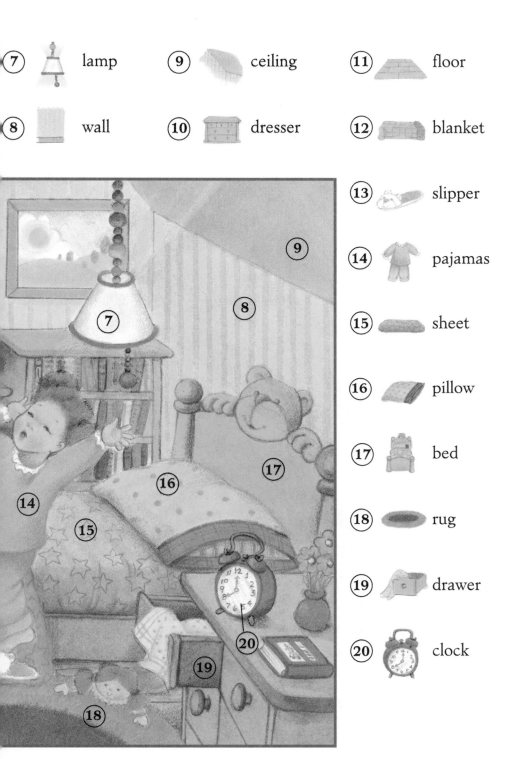

Toys

1. puzzle
2. game
3. teddy bear
4. stuffed animal
5. doll
6. dollhouse

(7) cards

(8) balloon

(9) toy truck

(10) drum

(11) blocks

(12) ball

(13) checkers

(14) action figure

(15) chess

(16) crayons

(17) easel

(18) paint

(19) marbles

(20) toy car

Bathroom

1. shower
2. shampoo
3. faucet
4. toilet
5. toilet paper
6. rubber duck

28

7 washcloth

9 bubbles

11 shower curtain

8 bathtub

10 bath mat

12 towel

13 towel rack

14 medicine cabinet

15 toothpaste

16 toothbrush

17 soap

18 soap dish

19 brush

20 comb

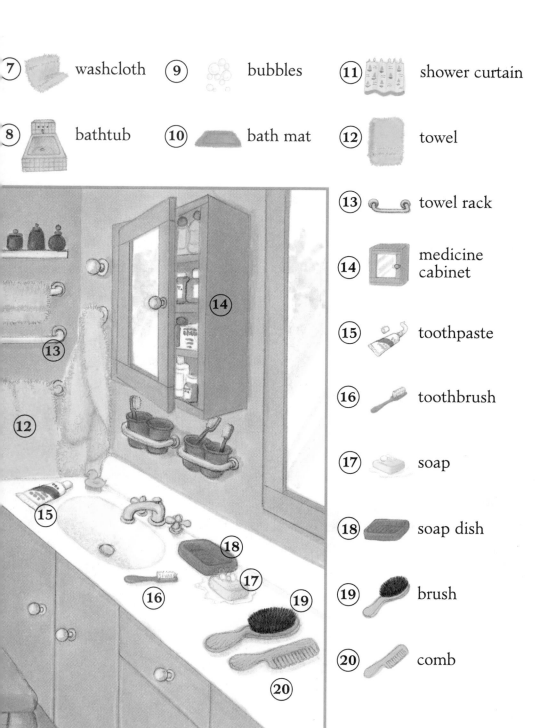

Living Room

① painting   ③ fireplace   ⑤ carpet

② fire   ④ steps   ⑥ bookcase

7 light

8 rocking chair

9 shelves

10 VCR

11 TV (television)

12 stereo

13 CDs (compact discs)

14 cassettes

15 curtains

16 plant

17 telephone

18 coffee table

19 vase

20 couch

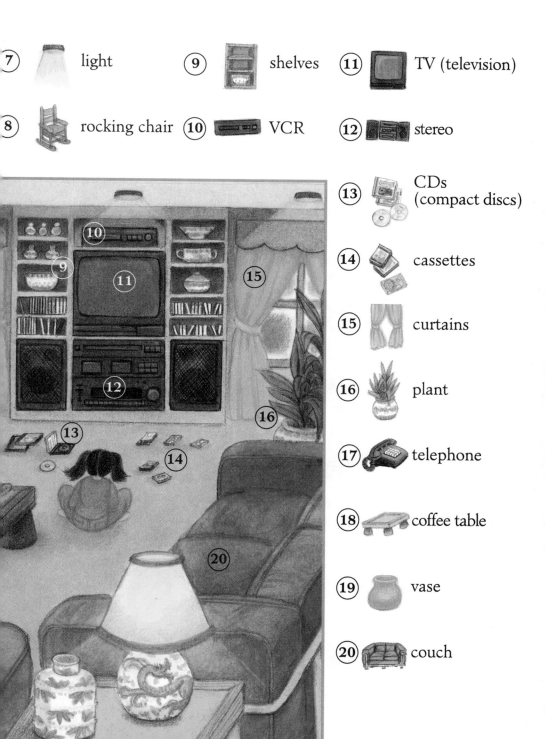

Kitchen

① broom   ③ freezer   ⑤ cabinet

② refrigerator   ④ counter   ⑥ toaster

(7) bowl (9) pot (11) stove

(8) sink (10) pan (12) oven

(13) glass

(14) cup

(15) saucer

(16) spoon

(17) knife

(18) plate

(19) napkin

(20) fork

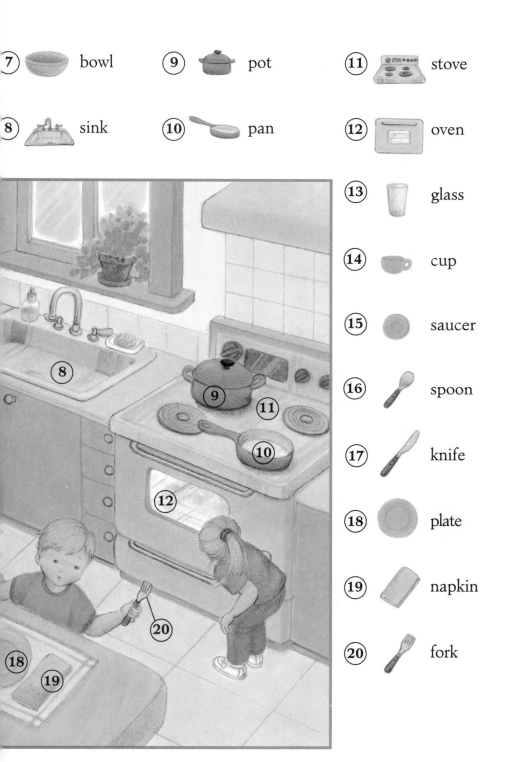

Food—Breakfast

 (1) strawberries   (3) butter   (5) banana

(2) cream cheese   (4) tomato   (6) milk

(7) oatmeal   (9) waffle   (11) orange juice

(8) sugar   (10) scrambled egg   (12) jam

(13) toast

(14) muffin

(15) pastry

(16) pancake

(17) egg

(18) bagel

(19) syrup

(20) cold cereal

Food—Lunch

1. potato chips
2. pretzels
3. peanut butter
4. jelly
5. cookies
6. bread

(7)  cheese

(8) straw

(9) soda

(10) hamburger

(11) cherries

(12) french fries

(13) crackers

(14) hot dog

(15) chocolate milk

(16) mustard

(17) ketchup

(18) sandwich

(19) apple

(20) apple juice

Food—Dinner

1 grapes   3 ice cube   5 pepper

2 orange   4 salt   6 cake

(7) beans

(9) meatballs

(11) fish

(8) salad

(10) spaghetti

(12) potato

(13) rice

(14) gravy

(15) soup

(16) roll

(17) carrot

(18) peas

(19) corn

(20) chicken leg

Classroom

1  picture   **3** colored pencil   **5** desk

2 book   **4** pencil   **6** pen

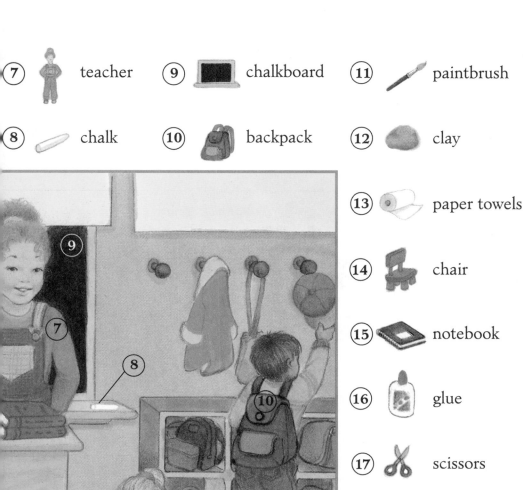

| 7 | teacher | 9 | chalkboard | 11 | paintbrush |
| 8 | chalk | 10 | backpack | 12 | clay |

13 paper towels

14 chair

15 notebook

16 glue

17 scissors

18 paper

19 marker

20 student

Neighborhood

1. house
2. restaurant
3. store
4. supermarket
5. bank
6. apartment building

(7) corner

(9) school bus

(11) library

(8) school

(10) sidewalk

(12) boy

(13) girl

(14) bus stop

(15) people

(16) garbage can

(17) street

(18) mailbox

(19) firehouse

(20) police station

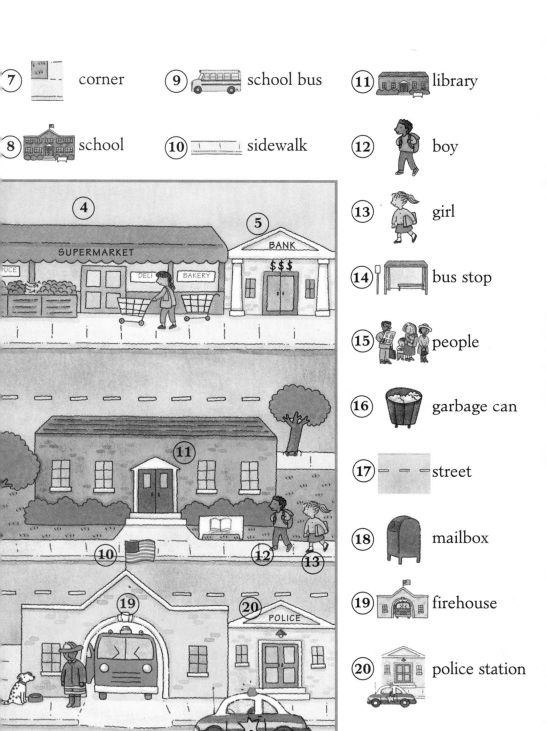

43

Supermarket

(1) frozen food (2) shopping cart (3) fruit

44

(4) aisle

(5) butcher

(6) meat

(7) candy

(8) vegetables

(9) broccoli

(10) spinach

(11) lettuce

(12) cash register

(13) cashier

(14) money

(15) paper bag

Transportation

(1) rocket

(3) airplane

(5) fire engine

(2) helicopter

(4) train

(6) van

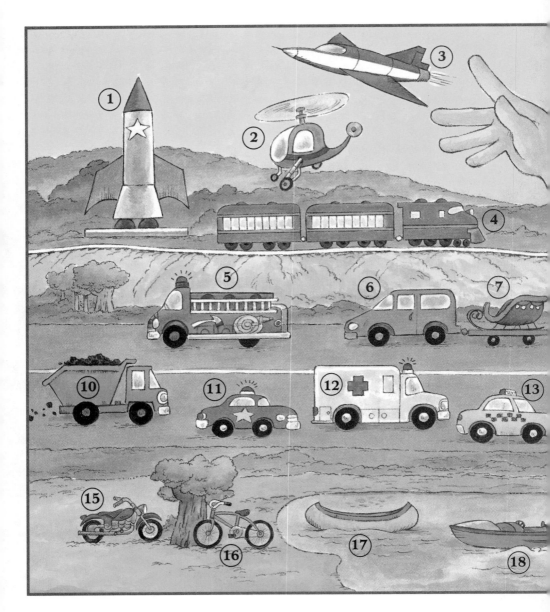

(7) sleigh

(8) car

(9) bus

(10) dump truck

(11) police car

(12) ambulance

(13) taxi

(14) tractor-trailer

(15) motorcycle

(16) bicycle

(17) canoe

(18) motorboat

(19) sailboat

(20) rowboat

Doctor's Office

48

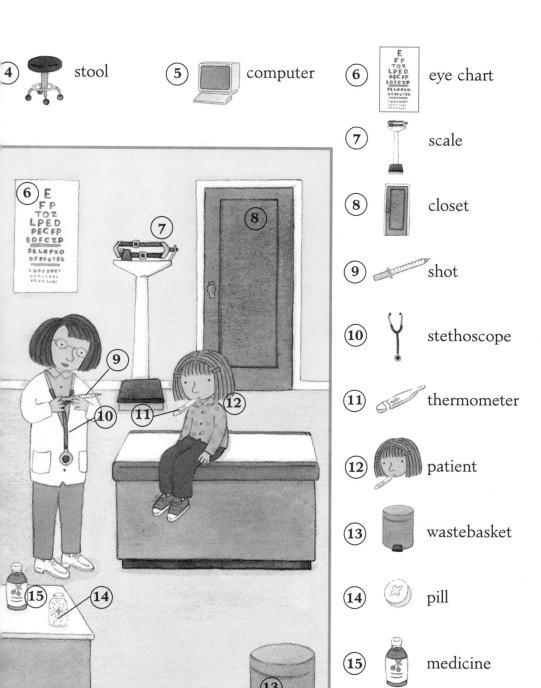

4 stool

5 computer

6 eye chart

7 scale

8 closet

9 shot

10 stethoscope

11 thermometer

12 patient

13 wastebasket

14 pill

15 medicine

49

Park

1. jungle gym
2. slide
3. tree
4. rock
5. swing
6. sandbox
7. seesaw
8. grass
9. water fountain
10. tricycle

51

At Play

1. push
2. run
3. pull
4. throw
5. climb
6. catch
7. walk
8. bend
9. jump rope
10. crawl

Sports

① hoop   ③ knee pads   ⑤ football

② basketball   ④ soccer ball   ⑥ tennis ball

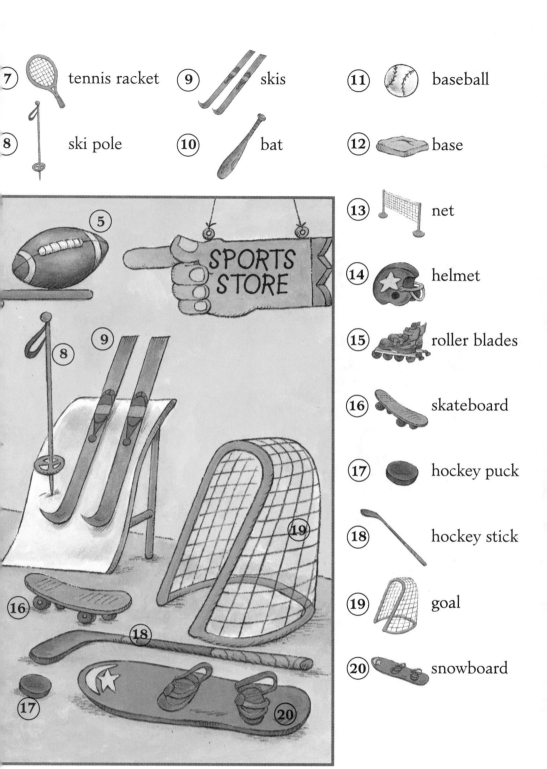

(7) tennis racket

(8) ski pole

(9) skis

(10) bat

(11) baseball

(12) base

(13) net

(14) helmet

(15) roller blades

(16) skateboard

(17) hockey puck

(18) hockey stick

(19) goal

(20) snowboard

SPORTS STORE

Workers

① train conductor　③ doctor　⑤ judge

② truck driver　④ reporter　⑥ cab driver

① ② ③ ④

⑧ ⑨ ⑩ ⑪

⑭ ⑮ ⑯ ⑰

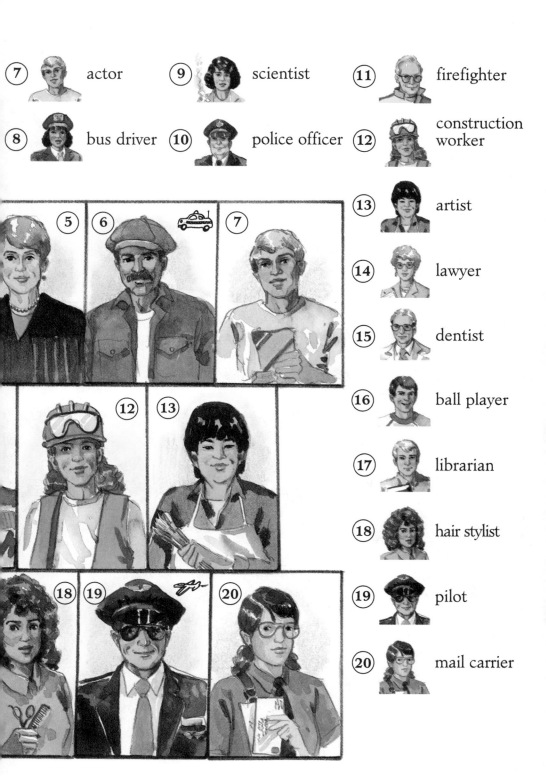

(7) actor

(9) scientist

(11) firefighter

(8) bus driver

(10) police officer

(12) construction worker

(13) artist

(14) lawyer

(15) dentist

(16) ball player

(17) librarian

(18) hair stylist

(19) pilot

(20) mail carrier

57

Pets

1. parrot
2. bird
3. goldfish
4. dog
5. cat
6. turtle
7. rabbit
8. guinea pig
9. hamster
10. gerbil

59

1  giraffe

2  kangaroo

3 camel

4  hippopotamus

5 elephant

6  zebra

7  bear

8  tiger

9  monkey

10  lion

61

Animals—2

1. fly
2. raccoon
3. fox
4. deer
5. snake
6. spider
7. wolf
8. chipmunk
9. mouse
10. skunk

1. seagull
2. sea turtle
3. fish
4. shrimp
5. octopus
6. crab
7. starfish
8. crocodile
9. frog
10. salamander

Animals—4

(1) horse   (2) crow   (3) pony

4 cow

5 calf

6 pig

7 goose

8 donkey

9 goat

10 chick

11 rooster

12 chicken

13 lamb

14 sheep

15 duck

Farm

1 field

3 scarecrow

5 silo

2 sky

4 wheat

6 hay

68

(7) barn

(8) farmhouse

(9) farmer

(10) dirt

(11) tractor

(12) wheelbarrow

(13) mud

(14) toolshed

(15) stable

(16) seed

(17) water

(18) pond

(19) pitchfork

(20) fence

Days, Weeks, Months

1

January

					1	2
3	4	5	6	7	8	9
10	11	12	13	14	15	16
17	18	19	20	21	22	23
24/31	25	26	27	28	29	30

2

February

1	2	3	4	5	6	
7	8	9	10	11	12	13
14	15	16	17	18	19	20
21	22	23	24	25	26	27
28						

4

April

			1	2	3	
4	5	6	7	8	9	10
11	12	13	14	15	16	17
18	19	20	21	22	23	24
25	26	27	28	29	30	

5

May

						1
2	3	4	5	6	7	8
9	10	11	12	13	14	15
16	17	18	19	20	21	22
23/30	24/31	25	26	27	28	29

7

July

			1	2	3	
4	5	6	7	8	9	10
11	12	13	14	15	16	17
18	19	20	21	22	23	24
25	26	27	28	29	30	31

8

August

1	2	3	4	5	6	7
8	9	10	11	12	13	14
15	16	17	18	19	20	21
22	23	24	25	26	27	28
29	30	31				

10

October

					1	2
3	4	5	6	7	8	9
10	11	12	13	14	15	16
17	18	19	20	21	22	23
24/31	25	26	27	28	29	30

11

November

1	2	3	4	5	6	
7	8	9	10	11	12	13
14	15	16	17	18	19	20
21	22	23	24	25	26	27
28	29	30				

March

③

	1	2	3	4	5	6
7	8	9	10	11	12	13
14	15	16	17	18	19	20
21	22	23	24	25	26	27
28	29	30	31			

June

⑥

		1	2	3	4	5
6	7	8	9	10	11	12
13	14	15	16	17	18	19
20	21	22	23	24	25	26
27	28	29	30			

September

⑨

			1	2	3	4
5	6	7	8	9	10	11
12	13	14	15	16	17	18
19	20	21	22	23	24	25
26	27	28	29	30		

December

⑫

			1	2	3	4
5	6	7	8	9	10	11
12	13	14	15	16	17	18
19	20	21	22	23	24	25
26	27	28	29	30	31	

⑬ Year

⑭ Sunday

⑮ Monday

⑯ Tuesday

⑰ Wednesday

⑱ Thursday

⑲ Friday

⑳ Saturday

Seasons—Fall

 ① leaf ② branch ③ tire

(4) sweatshirt (5) sweatpants (6) ghost costume

(7) skeleton costume

(8) watch

(9) turtleneck

(10) acorn

(11) squirrel

(12) pinecone

(13) sweater

(14) basket

(15) pumpkin

Seasons—Winter

 ① moon   ② earmuffs   ③ snowball

(4) snowman (5) hat

(6) mittens

(7) coat

(8) scarf

(9)  ice

(10) ski jacket

(11) boots

(12)  sled

(13) snow

(14) gloves

(15) ice skates

75

Seasons—Spring

①  rainbow   ② umbrella   ③ cloud

4 rain

5 watering can

6 puddle

7 sunflower

8 garden

9 tulip

10 rose

11 thorn

12 daisy

13 stem

14 flower petal

15 butterfly

Seasons—Summer

1  sun   2 wave   3 ocean

(4) beach   (5) lifeguard   (6) lifesaver

(7) sandcastle

(8) seashell

(9) pail

(10) bathing suits

(11) sand

(12) beach chair

(13) beach blanket

(14) sunglasses

(15) ice cream cone

At a Picnic

1. swim
2. cook
3. read
4. sleep
5. smell
6. laugh
7. drink
8. eat
9. pour
10. dance

Opposites—1

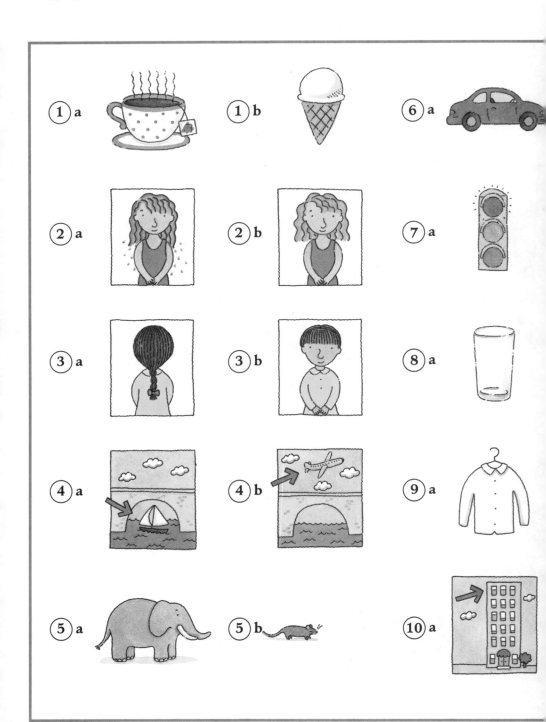

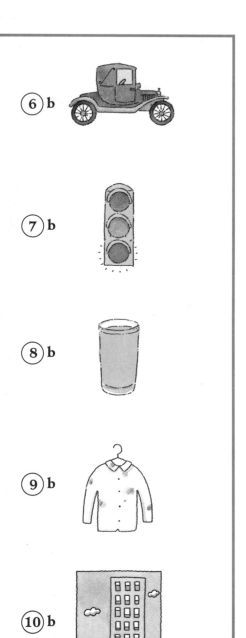

6 b

7 b

8 b

9 b

10 b

1 a	hot	**1** b	cold
2 a	wet	**2** b	dry
3 a	back	**3** b	front
4 a	below	**4** b	above
5 a	big	**5** b	little
6 a	new	**6** b	old
7 a	stop	**7** b	go
8 a	empty	**8** b	full
9 a	clean	**9** b	dirty
10 a	high	**10** b	low

Opposites—2

6 b

7 b

8 b

9 b

10 b

1 a fat   1 b thin

2 a alone   2 b together

3 a night   3 b day

4 a up   4 b down

5 a far   5 b near

6 a slow   6 b fast

7 a inside   7 b outside

8 a long   8 b short

9 a open   9 b closed

10 a over   10 b under

Index

	Page Number	Word Number		Page Number	Word Number
boots	75	11	cards	27	7
bowl	33	7	carpet	30	5
boy	43	12	carrot	39	17
branch	72	2	cash register	45	12
brave	19	7	cashier	45	13
bread	36	6	cassettes	31	14
breakfast	34		cast	48	2
broccoli	45	9	cat	59	5
broom	32	1	catch	53	6
brother	17	6	CDs (compact discs)	31	13
brown	15	2	ceiling	25	9
brush	29	19	chair	41	14
bubbles	29	9	chalk	41	8
bus	47	9	chalkboard	41	9
bus driver	57	8	checkers	27	13
bus stop	43	14	cheese	37	7
butcher	45	5	cherries	37	11
butter	34	3	chess	27	15
butterfly	77	15	chick	67	10
button	23	5	chicken	67	12
			chicken leg	39	20
			chipmunk	63	8
C c			chocolate milk	37	15
cab driver	56	6	classroom	40	
cabinet	32	5	clay	41	12
cake	38	6	clean	83	9a
calf	67	5	climb	53	5
calm	19	5	clock	25	20
camel	61	3	closed	85	9b
candy	45	7	closet	49	8
canoe	47	17	clothes	22	
cap	23	4	cloud	76	3
car	47	8	coat	75	7

	Page Number	Word Number		Page Number	Word Number
potato	39	12	rug	25	18
potato chips	36	1	run	53	2
pour	81	9			
pretzels	36	2			
proud	19	9	**S s**		
puddle	77	6	sad	19	2
pull	53	3	sailboat	47	19
pumpkin	73	15	salad	39	8
purple	15	6	salamander	65	10
push	53	1	salt	38	4
puzzle	26	1	sand	79	11
			sandbox	51	6
			sandcastle	79	7
R r			sandwich	37	18
rabbit	59	7	Saturday	71	20
raccoon	63	2	saucer	33	15
rain	77	4	scale	49	7
rainbow	76	1	scarecrow	68	3
read	81	3	scared	19	4
red	15	3	scarf	75	8
refrigerator	32	2	school	43	8
reporter	56	4	school bus	43	9
restaurant	42	2	scientist	57	9
rice	39	13	scissors	41	17
rock	51	4	scrambled egg	35	10
rocket	46	1	sea turtle	65	2
rocking chair	31	8	seagull	65	1
roll	39	16	seashell	79	8
roller blades	55	15	seasons	72	
rooster	67	11	seed	69	16
rose	77	10	seesaw	51	7
rowboat	47	20	September	71	9
rubber duck	28	6	seven	11	7

	Page Number	Word Number		Page Number	Word Number
tulip	**77**	9	watering can	**77**	5
turtle	**59**	6	wave	**78**	2
turtleneck	**73**	9	Wednesday	**71**	17
TV (television)	**31**	11	weeks	**70**	
twelve	**13**	12	wet	**83**	2a
twenty	**13**	20	wheat	**68**	4
two	**11**	2	wheelbarrow	**69**	12
			white	**15**	8
			window	**24**	6
			winter	**74**	
U u			wolf	**63**	7
umbrella	**76**	2	workers	**56**	
uncle	**17**	9			
under	**85**	10b			
up	**85**	4a			
			Y y		
			year	**71**	13
V v			yellow	**15**	4
van	**46**	6			
vase	**31**	19			
VCR	**31**	10	**Z z**		
vegetables	**45**	8	zebra	**61**	6
vest	**23**	14			

W w

waffle	**35**	9
walk	**53**	7
wall	**25**	8
washcloth	**29**	7
wastebasket	**49**	13
watch	**73**	8
water	**69**	17
water fountain	**51**	9

Hello Reader! Sight Words

a	is	saw
am	look	see
and	make	she
are	me	the
come	no	to
go	not	too
has	of	under
he	on	was
I	or	we